IMAGES
of America

MANTECA

Pictured is the track of the future Southern Pacific Railroad, which was completed in 1870. The alignment bisected the heart of downtown and the property of Joshua Cowell, the "Father of Manteca." (Courtesy of Manteca Historical Society and Museum.)

On the Cover: The first blacksmith shop was located on the southwest corner of Yosemite and Maple Avenues, prior to moving to the 100 block of North Main Street. The operation was under the ownership of R.E. Leventon and Son. R.E. Leventon Sr. served on the chamber of commerce in the 1920s. (Courtesy of Manteca Historical Society and Museum.)

IMAGES
of America

MANTECA

Melinda Pacheco Patrick

ARCADIA
PUBLISHING

ISBN 978-1-4671-0418-0

Published by Arcadia Publishing
Charleston, South Carolina

Printed in the United States of America

Library of Congress Control Number: 2019940809

For all general information, please contact Arcadia Publishing:
Telephone 843-853-2070
Fax 843-853-0044
E-mail sales@arcadiapublishing.com
For customer service and orders:
Toll-Free 1-888-313-2665

Visit us on the Internet at www.arcadiapublishing.com

This book is dedicated to Evelyn Prouty and Ken Hafer, keepers of history.

Contents

Acknowledgments

This book would not have been possible without the definitive work of Evelyn Prouty, who penned *Manteca: Selected Chapters from Its History* (1980). It is her research and writing that serves as the backbone of this book. In addition, I took inspiration from the first book written about the town, Alice B. Coon's *Manteca: The Story of a Town* (1943).

I am ever so grateful to the late Ken Hafer. During my research for this book, I cannot count the number of times I heard the following words: "You know who would know is Ken Hafer." Hafer was essential in establishing the museum in the early 1990s; however, the origins of the museum began decades before with archives and collections he privately housed. He took great pride in his hometown and was passionate about sharing history, as evidenced in every nook and cranny of the museum.

Many thanks to the Manteca Historical Society and Museum and the generous donors who have filled every inch of space with priceless photographs and heirlooms. I am ever so thankful to the board and docents who contribute their time in keeping the history alive and accessible to the public. I would like to extend my gratitude to Sally Mendes, Ericka Mendes Meadows, and Jeanette Farley for fact-checking and editing. In particular, I'd like to thank Mike Brockman and Jeanette Farley for lifting my spirits and going out of their way to assist me. Unless otherwise noted, all images appearing in this book were provided by the Manteca Historical Society and Museum.

To each and every one of you who shared a story and provided input, your efforts are appreciated. Off the top of my head, these individuals include my father, Chester Pacheco; Art Perry; Gary Alfieri; Lucille Harris; and Chris Teicheira. I would like to thank my mother, Patricia (Morris) Eavenson, who tirelessly helped scan photographs and solve mysteries; my daughters, Lela and Elsie, who kept me smiling with their encouragement; and my son, Everett, for sharing my love of history and being my photographer. Lastly, my husband, Ian, is due buckets of gratitude for editing photographs and text, embarking on wild goose chases and last-minute missions of impossibility, and simply loving me through the process.

INTRODUCTION

The Central Valley has been home to indigenous populations for approximately 13,000 years. The first inhabitants developed an elaborate material culture and trade network, combined with remarkable village sizes and population densities, comparable only to agricultural societies of the southwest and southeast. When Europeans arrived, approximately 100,000 people occupied the Central Valley, composing one-third of California's native population. Manteca lies within the ethnographic aboriginal territory of the Northern Valley Yokut (yōkut). Prior to urbanization, the valley floor was a vast plain consisting of a network of wetlands, sloughs, tributaries, and natural levees, with thick tule marshes surrounded by sparsely populated grassland dotted with valley oaks. Riparian woodlands dominated the streams and rivers with sycamores, cottonwoods, and willows. The valley environment provided a rich habitat for wildlife, including fish, mussels, turtles, birds, waterfowl, tule elks, pronghorn antelope, rabbits, squirrels, beavers, and quail.

The Northern Valley Yokut organized into tribes of approximately 300 people, establishing villages and hamlets along waterways on elevated mounds. Villages consisted of single-family dwellings covered in tule mats, a sweathouse, and a ceremonial assembly chamber. The Yokut were hunters and gatherers, exploiting the wetlands and nearby riverine and oak savanna environments, while engaging in a dynamic exchange system with their neighbors to the west along the coast and to the east with the foothill tribes. After 1770, the Yokut way of life was disrupted by the influx of Spanish colonial expeditions and missionaries in search of converts. Introduced diseases, in particular the 1833 malaria epidemic, claimed thousands of lives, and it is estimated that 75 percent of the valley population was lost by 1846. Beginning in 1848, settlers and miners spurred on by the gold rush displaced the Yokut from their land. This series of events led to the erosion of their culture and decimation of their population.

In 1806, Spanish lieutenant Gabriel Moraga passed through the valley on his way north along the San Joaquin River, giving both the river and the county their names. On the heels of Moraga, members of the Hudson's Bay Company and other trappers and traders camped along the rivers. Amongst them was Jedediah Smith in 1827, the first American to come overland to California. On his second expedition, Lt. John C. Frémont of the US Topographical Corps passed through the Manteca area.

In 1846, a small group of Mormons launched the first vessel to sail upriver from the Bay, landing near Mossdale. They continued upriver and established the first colony in San Joaquin County, New Hope, a short-lived agricultural settlement where the Stanislaus and San Joaquin Rivers converge.

The discovery of gold on the American River in 1848 sparked the great westward expansion. Settlers began to arrive in earnest in the 1850s, some seeking their fortune in the Mother Lode, while others sought to improve their circumstances through other pursuits, including agriculture. Many of the early pioneers came from Grants County, Wisconsin, including the "Father of Manteca," Joshua Cowell. Cowell came west in 1861, settling land in the heart of what is now downtown Manteca. At one time, he owned 1,000 acres and rented another 1,000 acres. Cowell's ranch garnered a two-page illustrated spread in Thomas H. Thompson and Albert A. West's *History of San Joaquin County* (1879).

In 1869, a momentous event took place when the last link in the Transcontinental Railroad connected the East Coast with the West Coast. The railroad was vital to the city's development, unlocking agricultural and economic potential. During the 1870s, the Central Valley became a network of rail lines connecting communities in an unprecedented way. In 1870, the Western Pacific (future Southern Pacific) Railroad completed the section of railway from Stockton to the Stanislaus River, bisecting Manteca. It was at this time that the name Manteca was given to the town. As the story goes, another stop down the line was known as Cowell Station. In order to avoid confusion, Monteca (an adaptation of the Spanish word for butter, *mantequilla*) was proposed. Whether by accident or intentionally, the Southern Pacific printed Manteca (Spanish for lard) on the tickets, and the name remained.

Early irrigation in the late 1890s provided farmers with the vision of what could be achieved, and the dairy industry was born. However, it was the completion of the irrigation network in 1914, rallied by Cowell, that propelled Manteca into the future. The South San Joaquin Irrigation District (SSJID) brought water to 70,000 acres. Large wheat ranches subdivided, small rural farms emerged, and real estate boomed. The board of trade printed pamphlets touting 150 crops that could be grown here, giving us the name of "District of Diversified Crops." San Joaquin Valley outpaced the state in farm population at this time; SSJID records indicate cultivation skyrocketed from 15,539 acres in 1909 to 51,095 acres in 1915.

A combination of the railroad and irrigation brought on large-scale production with the Spreckels Sugar Company and the Manteca Canning Company. These two industries responded to the supply and demand brought on by World War I. Spreckels sugar beets were the answer to the sugar shortage, and the Manteca Canning Company was the realization of four notable townsmen addressing the need to process the large quantities of produce.

Manteca suffered in the 1920s and 1930s, first with the drought in 1924, which brought on catastrophic shortages in crops, followed by hoof-and-mouth disease, which decimated the dairy population. The latter decade could be characterized by events brought on by the Depression and the Dust Bowl. Spreckels initially closed due to a diseased sugar beet crop, resulting in lost jobs, and Midwesterners came by the thousands, lowering local wages. Labor strife was a major issue, the first flood of the 20th century happened in 1930, and fires ravaged the town. Happier times were on the horizon when Spreckels introduced a disease-resistant seed, and the sugar beet crop of 1939 was record breaking. The Department of Agriculture began a program to help farmers, volunteers rallied to make the last payment on the La France fire engine, and the Manteca Library Association was formed.

Like many other cities, Manteca weathered World War II despite the labor shortages and the economic downturn. Victorious soldiers returned home, beginning the baby boom, and Spreckels production went through the roof in the latter part of the 1940s. The 1950s ushered in a golden era of tranquility despite floods and fires between 1951 and 1952. The 1960s saw an explosion of community and industry, including expansion of Spreckels and the post office, construction of new churches, and completion of the library.

The latter part of the 20th century saw a disparity between pro-growth and anti-growth sentiments as Manteca became a bedroom community for the Bay Area. The right-to-farm ordinance and a set of regulations attempted to curb the consumption of farmland and mindfully direct the expansion. Today, Manteca has grown to a population of around 80,000. The town has a high-tech sector, distribution centers, and big-box stores, along with Big League Dreams, Bass Pro Shop, and the Great Wolf Lodge. However, Manteca still has a strong economic grounding in agriculture, primarily dairy, grapes, and almonds. In 2018, the city of Manteca celebrated its centennial.

One

TRAILBLAZERS
PIONEERS AND LEADERS

The overland trip out West was not for the faint of heart. The terrain was rugged, there were no amenities, babies were born, loved ones died, and shear survival weighed on everyone's minds. The Salmon wagon train took six months to make the journey. Upon arrival, they (like many others) made the split decision to go to California rather than Oregon (their original destination). Many of the early settlers who came to the area were from Grants County, Wisconsin, including Salmon, Reynolds, Graves, Castle, Harelson, and Oliver. When they arrived, there was no semblance of the present-day town.

When the Reynolds family left Grant County in 1853, they traveled between 12 and 15 miles per day along the Emigrant Trail. They paused once for childbirth and again to lighten the load after three of their horses died from drinking alkali water. They left behind prized possessions, including five quilts, a feather bed, cooking utensils, a keg of syrup, and a gun. According to Evelyn Prouty's *Manteca: Selected Chapters from Its History*, the pile of goods was left with a sign that read "Help yourself."

Another couple from Grant County, Elijah and Sarah Bowers Harelson, arrived in 1864. It took a year to prepare for the trip, including curing meats, gathering medicinal herbs, creating a cracker barrel, and drying beans and potatoes. The wagon train consisted of 68 wagons. At times, they traveled with handkerchiefs stuffed in the mouths of children to gain ground from the Native Americans under the cover of night.

Once here, there was little in the way of life and order these settlers were accustomed to. The West was full of new experiences. According to historical accounts of the Castle family, the children would be ushered inside when the Native Americans watered their stock at the ranch. The children would watch in awe from chinks in the walls of the cabin. George Castle served as sheriff in San Joaquin County during a murder trial, and apparently, pieces of the murderer's hide were handed out after he was hung, skinned, and tanned. And vigilante-style justice was meted out as settlers took matters into their own hands; for example, in the 1850s, the men in town had a "talk" with a man who repeatedly abused his wife. The man disappeared and was never to be seen again, according to Elwyn Arnold.

Cutler Salmon was born in New York in 1809. He married Janet "Jane" Reynolds from Grant County, Wisconsin, in 1829, and they had 10 children. In 1853, he was appointed captain of the wagon train headed west based on his experience in the Black Hawk War. The group took the Emigrant Trail and arrived in Hangtown, currently Placerville, after the six-month journey.

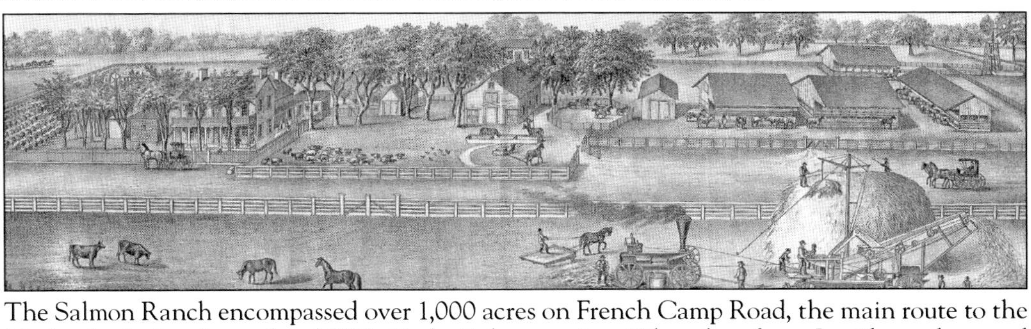

The Salmon Ranch encompassed over 1,000 acres on French Camp Road, the main route to the Mother Lode. In a letter dated 1853, Cutler Salmon writes, "I bought a farm. I paid one thousand dollars for it . . . Was offered three thousand for my bargain . . . Would not take ten thousand for it. I think if there is a place in California that would suit me, this will."

These photographs show the house and barn at the Salmon Ranch, also known as Dutch Point. This location was the site of an 1849 public house and stage stop owned by two settlers, Benniden and Jenks. The owners, Dutchmen anxious to head to the gold country and make their fortune, sold to Salmon, who continued to operate the hotel on the property. At that time, French Camp was a hub of travel and trade. Boats navigated the slough from the Bay Area and Stockton, where people and goods unloaded and traveled via wagon to the gold mines. The house was built in 1866 with bricks made on the property by John Reynolds. In 1883, workers hit a deposit of swamp gas, which was piped into the house for lighting and cooking. This domestic use of "tule gas" may have been the first in the state.

George Castle, who heralded from New York, and Harriet Oliver, of Wisconsin, married in 1846. They had 14 children, only nine of whom survived infancy. The family came overland to California, crossing the Mississippi River in 1852, and arrived in Hangtown (now Placerville). For much of the journey, George carried his daughter due to her poor health. George served as sheriff in San Joaquin County during the gold rush era, when immigration and murder were rampant and communication was scarce.

The Castle homestead is located on French Camp Road. The first home was a simple cabin measuring 12 by 12 feet, with a tool chest for a table and green hides for a roof. When describing his original home, George Castle said that when he "put down the carpet of gunny sacks, he felt himself quite extravagant." This photograph shows the home that replaced the cabin.

This illustration from Thompson and West's 1879 book depicts George Castle's Standardbred horses being worked at the racetrack across from the 10-room house built of redwood and hand-forged nails. A 1870 single-seater sulky belonging to the Castles, as illustrated here, was donated to the San Joaquin County Historical Museum.

This photograph of the Reynolds brothers (ranging from 70 to 82 years old) was taken in 1914. From left to right are Edward, Richard, James, David, and Eldridge. These men were the sons of Martha Ramsey and James Reynolds Sr., who came west in 1853 along with one daughter; another daughter crossed the plains two years prior. This family farmed land between Yosemite Avenue and French Camp Road.

The home of Eldridge Reynolds was located on North Union Road (originally Reynolds Road). Eldridge and his brother Edward operated a wheat thresher for area farmers in addition to their own 1,000 acres. Eldridge caught his leg in the thresher, eventually having it amputated and buried. He complained of a cramp in his toe, so the leg was dug up, the toe straightened, and the pain ceased.

Henrietta Reynolds (white sleeves) is seen out with friends, including James Barr (with the beard), enjoying the river in 1890. Barr became the San Joaquin County school superintendent. Henrietta, David Reynolds's daughter, was essential in restoring the declining East Union Cemetery and raising the entrance arch dedicated to the pioneers. Henrietta authored *Pioneers of the Sand Plain* and donated countless items to the Pioneer Museum in Stockton.

The original Reynolds Road bisected the Reynolds ranches to access the home of their uncle Cutler Salmon. Eldridge Reynolds is photographed here with his first car. His brother David befriended a fellow Argonaut in Hangtown who made wheelbarrows for miners. David was happy with the wheelbarrow, and when the man started making cars, David bought one, saying, "He made good wheelbarrows, he must make good cars." That man was John M. Studebaker.

Elijah and Sarah Bowers Harelson, another couple from Grant County, Wisconsin, followed their daughter, who was engaged to marry David Reynolds. Elijah had previously made the trip and worked the mines. In 1864, the wagon train arrived in California. The family purchased property on French Camp Road. Sarah was a midwife and doctored children. (Courtesy of Everett Patrick.)

Leaving Massachusetts in 1849, Peter Clapp was successful in the Jamestown–Poverty Hill mining area and opened a butcher shop. Traveling through Manteca, he realized he could harvest wood and send it to the Stockton area for fuel. He purchased property at Main Street and Louise Avenue. His brother Noah and Noah's wife, Louisa, followed, settling near New Haven School. The current Louise Avenue is named after her. (Courtesy of Everett Patrick.)

Capt. John McMullin, born in 1824 in Maryland, ran away and joined the Texas Rangers at 15. During the Mexico and Texas conflict, he was captured. On his second escape attempt, he showed such bravery that the Mexicans stopped fighting, applauded, and allowed the prisoners to escape. Upon hearing this, General Santa Anna of Mexico sent McMullin a silver belt. McMullin was lured to California by gold fever; however, shortly after, he and his partner realized cattle were a better prospect. He eventually amassed 30,000 acres, including Casa Blanca near the confluence of the San Joaquin and Stanislaus Rivers, where he lived with his wife, Eliza, and their nine children.

After leaving their home in Maine, Jesse A. and Mary Wentworth Austin arrived in California via the Isthmus of Panama around 1852. They acquired 640 acres near Highway 120 and Austin Road. They had three sons and one daughter. Their first home, which was constructed where Calla School stands, was moved to 160 acres held by their daughter, Inez. The second home, pictured here, consisted of 13 rooms and is still standing and occupied on Austin Road. Taken in 1886, this photograph shows, from left to right, son-in-law E.N. Pierce holding baby Edna, Jesse A. Austin, his wife Mary Austin, grandson J. Austin Pierce, and daughter Inez A. Pierce.

Inez Austin married Edward N. Pierce, who traveled west in 1880. He became the first secretary of the SSJID before taking on the role of head nurse at the San Joaquin General Hospital. Inez and Edward N. Pierce are seated with their children (from left to right) Chester, Ned, Effie, Austin, Edna, Bryan, Lela, and Mark. The banner Inez is holding depicts four stars to represent her four sons serving in the military during World War I.

E.N. Pierce (standing far right) is seen on holiday in 1909 with a group on its way to the Cliff House in San Francisco.

Effie S. Pierce, assistant secretary of the SSJID, is pictured here in 1914. Decked out in the current fashion, Effie boards the car of Henry Lutge, SSJID civil engineer. She married George D. Murphy Sr. of the *Manteca Bulletin*.

Four of the most influential men in the development of Manteca are pictured here: from left to right, Achille Baccilieri, Benjamin A. Goodwin, Joshua Cowell, and George Weatherbee.

This c. 1890 portrait is of the Joshua Cowell family. Standing are the children from his first marriage to Vinnette Rachael Graves: from left to right, Clara C. (married J. Clifford Wiggin), Mary E. (married Charles L. Salmon), Elida A. (married James V. Salmon), and Otis (married Elsie Harrington). Seated are Joshua and his second wife, Emily F. Sanders Cowell, and their daughter Hattie V. (married M.H. Mewborn).

The Cowell home consisted of 10 or 11 rooms and stood at the corner of Yosemite Avenue and Main Street. Joshua and his second wife, Emily, are pictured with their granddaughter Ollie Salmon (far right) and her friend Mary Coykendall.

In 1861, Joshua Cowell traveled west with his brothers, staying behind in Nevada for two years before trekking the Sierra Nevada by foot. He settled in the heart of what became downtown Manteca. The first home was moved to the ranch, and it was in this house that all of his children were born. In 1904, a new home was constructed with six bedrooms, a dining room, a living room, two bathrooms, and a parlor.

Pioneer families united at the Salmon and Cowell double wedding on October 8, 1890. Pictured here are the newlyweds, James Vincent Salmon and Elida Almeda Cowell (the couple at left) and Charles Leslie Salmon and Mary Edna Cowell.

Here, Benjamin Goodwin is posing with his bike around 1869. In 1904, Goodwin, the "Father of the Irrigation District," invented a leveling instrument that was used to construct over 200 miles of canals. When he passed away in 1930, the stores in both Ripon and Manteca closed for an hour out of respect.

This 1897 photograph depicts the Goodwin family: from left to right, Elmer, Nellie May, Mary, Alfred D., Benjamin, Irvin, and Arthur. Goodwin arrived in California around the age of 16, traveling with his family via the Isthmus of Panama. Not long after, he purchased 160 acres on Highway 120, eventually adding another 160 acres. He married Mary E. Clapp in 1879.

The Goodwin home, built in 1895, was located on East Highway 120. The first home was repurposed as a blacksmith shop. The family raised grain prior to transitioning into almonds and dairy. Mary made butter to trade for staples in Stockton, where they traveled weekly to get mail. Highwaymen would hide out in the oak grove near French Camp Slough, and Ben was once held up during a trip.

Nellie May Goodwin is pictured here on her wedding day to Laurence Lee "L.L." Miller in 1906. Miller was a farmer and inventor. The couple owned property on East Yosemite Avenue.

Born in New York in 1856, George Wetherbee left home at the age of 21, seeking his fortune in California. Landing in Manteca, he worked for a local farmer (likely Marion Cowell). He married Eva Litchfield in 1883. The land along Bronzan Road near Oakwood and Weatherbee Lakes was once the family farm. They are pictured here with their children, Clarence H. and Edna L., in 1898.

Walter E. Woodward arrived in Manteca in 1905 and married Fannie Scherrer. He farmed 160 acres near Airport Way and Woodward Avenue, ran a real estate venture with E.E. Douglass, and served on the irrigation board. (Courtesy of Walter E. Woodward School.)

Henry Benton Graves was born on January 14, 1810, in Culpepper, Virginia, and married Lurena Howell of Virginia. They were the parents of 12 children, including Vinnette Rachael, who married Joshua Cowell, and Ada Elizabeth, who married F. Marion Cowell.

James Walter and Carrie Smith Graves (his second wife) are pictured here on their wedding day in 1885. J. Walter, as he was known, came overland with his parents from Grant County, Wisconsin, in 1864 at the age of 11. His first wife, Emma Liesy of French Camp, died in 1883, leaving behind two sons. Another son was born of his second union. J. Walter joined the sheriff's department in 1890, opened the Irrigation District Land Company, aided in finalizing the irrigation system, served as chairman of the commonwealth committee and the board of trade, and became the constable of Castoria Township when the town incorporated. He was known for his work ethic and kindness, remembered as the man who returned bicycles, found lost dogs, and gave kids a ride home in the rain.

Four of the sons of Henry and Lurena Graves, pictured here in 1868, are Newton Harvey, James Walter, Thomas Benton, and Francis Andrew.

John and Lucy Graves McKenzie traveled in the wagon train led by Cutler Salmon, along with the Harelson, Reynolds, and Graves families. They are pictured here in 1890 by the hitching post in front of their home on North Main Street (originally known as McKenzie Road).

E.E. Douglass began in real estate in Manteca in the early 1900s in partnership with Walter E. Woodward. He won the position of justice of the peace in 1918 and became a lawyer in 1923. He served in both capacities until 1952. From left to right in this 1923 family photograph are (first row) Donald and Frances; (second row) Dorothea, E.E., and Ada.

The Douglass home at 111 North Veach Street is pictured here. Judge Douglass was born in Vermont in 1886. At the age of 21, his father gave him $125 and urged him to travel west with his uncle.

Jesse Jerome "J.J." and Rosaella Sylvina "Vina" Overshiner arrived in California in 1883. J.J. worked for Joshua Cowell and purchased land from him. The first home built was moved to the corner of Willow Avenue and Oak Street to accommodate their second home at 629 West Yosemite Avenue. Their property stretched from the Southern Pacific Railroad tracks to Union Road; eventually, the Overshiners subdivided and sold lots through Douglass and Woodward Real Estate.

A daughter of J.J. and Vina, Jessie E. Overshiner Crane is pictured here around 1920 in front of the family home. Ollie and Pat Cotrell later owned the home at 629 West Yosemite Avenue, which is still standing and occupied.

In 1904, Ed Powers arrived by bicycle via train tracks from Lathrop and rented 80 acres from Joshua Cowell. In addition to farming, Powers sat on the board of trade, started the first telephone system, rallied for schools to be erected, and was responsible for Spreckels establishing its beet factory here.

This is the home of Ed Powers at 614 West Yosemite Avenue. Powers became the "Watermelon King of California" due to his deep cultivation methods in the depleted soils, producing enough watermelons after a few years to earn Manteca the name "Watermelon Capital of the World." Powers continued farming until he operated 27 ranches and had several warehouses near the railroad tracks. (Courtesy of Everett Patrick.)

Congressman John Joseph McFall (right) is pictured here with Pres. John F. Kennedy. McFall graduated from Manteca High School in 1934 and attended the University of California, Berkeley. After serving in World War II, he became mayor of Manteca. In 1951, he was elected to the California Assembly. He was appointed to the US Congress in 1956 and acted as both the floor and majority whips. He also served on the House Committee on Appropriations and the Defense Subcommittee.

Two

Schools and Churches
Shaping Minds and Hearts

In the early days of settlements, schools and churches served as community hubs for social gatherings. Generally, these buildings began as one-room wooden structures with a wood-burning stove. They were multifunctional, housing town hall meetings, church services, dances, funerals, and schools. Throughout the annals of history, these buildings often succumbed to fire.

Initially, Castoria Township was divided into four school districts in 1855: Castle, French Camp, Tulare (Lathrop), and Union. Construction on Castle and Union commenced that same year, and Lathrop began construction in 1857. French Camp had been operating since 1851 and is the oldest school in the county. In 1852, it cost on average $24.55 per child per year, and the teacher's salary was $60 per month.

One of the most notable events involves James, Eldridge, and Edward Reynolds, who attended French Camp School. In 1828, French trappers camped on the bank of French Camp Slough, and they continued a colony there until 1845. In 1856, the Reynolds boys found an abandoned cache of swords buried in the schoolyard, remnants of the French colony. Three of these are on display at the museum in Stockton.

One church was built in the 19th century, the Union Church. Initially, the congregation shared the Union School; however, funerals caused quite a disturbance to classes being held at the same time, and so a separate facility was erected on the southeast corner of the intersection of Union Road and Louise Avenue.

It was not until the first decade of the 20th century, coinciding with the population boom brought about by irrigation, that additional churches were constructed. The Union Chapel was constructed on the corner of Sycamore Avenue and North Street. Around 1910, Union Chapel was shared by the Brethren, Methodist, Congregational, and Christian congregations. The chapel was awarded first place in the county for its efficiency in sharing the facility as well as holding a multidenominational Sunday school. The Ladies Aid Society rallied fund-raisers for the church, including serving supper with strawberries and cream, hot biscuits, cake, and tea for 25¢ on the front lawn of Joshua Cowell's home in 1913.

The original one-story French Camp School, built in 1850, was used as a town hall and community center. The Sons of Temperance added the second story for use as a church. Records from 1852 document enrollment of 91 students; however, only eight attended on average. The building burned in the 1890s, and an elaborate Queen Anne was erected (pictured here). As enrollment grew, a new brick building was built in 1927.

French Camp is the oldest school in San Joaquin County. This photograph is of the class of 1922–1923 standing on the steps of the Queen Anne–style school. French Camp was a very diversified community, as evidenced in this photograph depicting several Japanese American students.

Originally a one-room school constructed on land donated by William Harelson and George Castle, Castle School provided an education for children traveling up to 10 miles one way. A second school followed the same year and another in 1924. The photograph above is the building from 1874, and the photograph below depicts the last Castle School serving the district. In 1932, the teacher, Olive Taylor, spanked a student. Later that afternoon, the janitor heard noises, and he entered the room to see the angry father of the child shoot and kill Taylor. The janitor was injured in the face during the altercation. The father's car was found burning, and the man fled to his homeland of Greece. When he returned to the United States, he could not be arrested for some unknown legal statute. The incident brought national notoriety.

Built in 1875 on I Street, the Lathrop School had 57 students enrolled in 1879. Ethel Ryhiner recalled the school vibrating when the strong winds blew through the open landscape, creating sand storms that would lead to school closures. In 1916, a new school was built, and trees were planted in memory of Viola Reynolds Ryhiner upon her death in 1930.

Union School, located on Airport Way and established in 1857, relocated to the northeast corner of Union Road and Louise Avenue, becoming East Union. This photograph, taken in either 1883 or 1894, depicts students and members of the community. The building housed church meetings, funerals, and dances.

This photograph shows the East Union class of 1881. Several boys are seen holding baseball bats, and two holes in the window look like missed fly balls! A fire destroyed the building in 1913.

Zinc House School, originally a hotel and stage stop on Highway 120 and Wagner Road, was roofed and clad in rare sheets of zinc. Ernest Wagener purchased the property in 1852, hiring a tutor for his 10 children and others in the area. A new school was established in 1861 on French Camp Road, seen here around 1890, using the same name. It became known as Atlanta in 1915.

Horses were a common mode of transportation for students. According to Sarah Von Klompenburg of Atlanta, children were allowed to bring their guns to school, storing them near the teacher's desk during the day, so they could hunt or shoot on their way home. In 1879, fifty-six students were enrolled. This c. 1890 photograph is in front of Zinc House School (Atlanta).

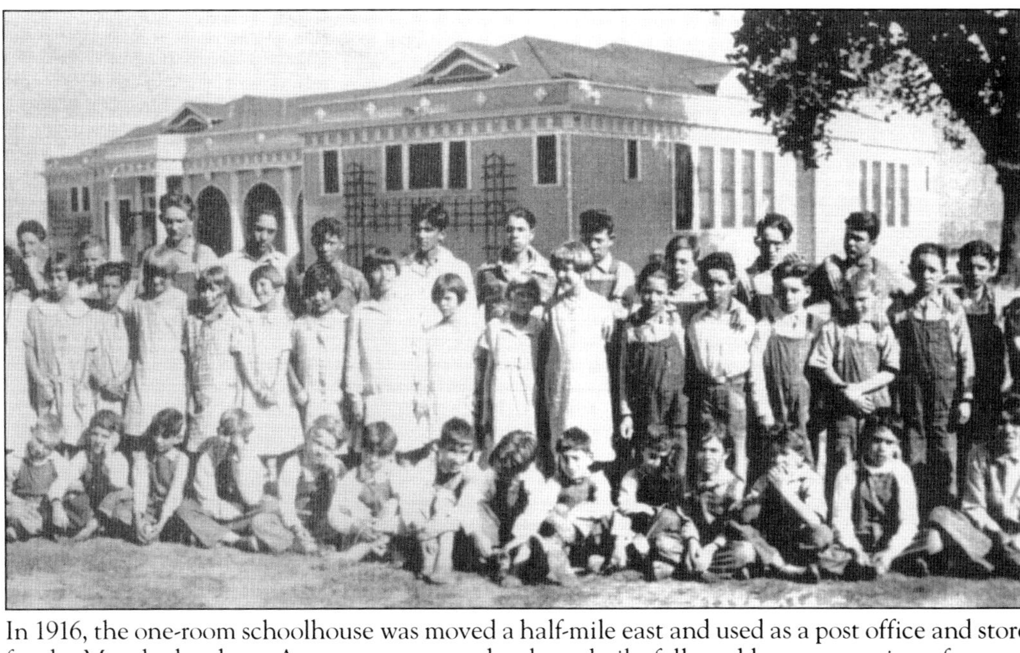

In 1916, the one-room schoolhouse was moved a half-mile east and used as a post office and store for the Murphy brothers. A new one-room school was built, followed by construction of a stage and auditorium. The Atlanta School closed its doors in 1971, and children began attending New Haven or Ripon.

Rustic School opened in 1870 on Airport Way (Durham Ferry) with 30 students and a barn for horses. Two boys were required to stand inside for most of the winter after they blew up the firewood supply, and another story tells of a child who tossed gunpowder into the stove, filling the room with soot and collapsing the pipe. The new school pictured was erected in 1920.

Mossdale School was built in 1898 on old Highway 120 to accommodate the increasing population. The school was built up to avoid floods, and children used the Mossdale ferry to get to school. Prior to construction of the one-room schoolhouse, children attended class in an abandoned chicken coop of Joe Lawrence. A new building was erected in 1954 before closing its doors in 1966.

Calla School was built in 1901 on the corner of Austin Road and Highway 120. In 1913, the school was the first in the district to boast "open-air" portable classrooms, consisting of board floors with canvas tents and heated with a stove. The school, replaced in 1918, burned in 1934, and classes continued in tents until the replacement structure was built with money borrowed from the Public Works Administration.

Summer Home School was built in 1906 on the corner of Cottage Avenue and Southland Road. Men leveled the land and built a playground in 1912. The school operated until the trustees purchased property on Austin Road to build New Haven School in 1957, combining Summer Home District with Castle District. Summer Home was demolished and the parcel returned to a relative of the donor.

In 1912, a total of 30 students attended school in rented space within the board of trade building, and by 1914, over 1,000 students were attending and overcrowding the 13 regional schools. Yosemite School (above) opened its doors in 1914 on three acres donated by J.J. Overshiner on West Yosemite Avenue, including a barn and restrooms relocated from East Union School, which burned down. In 1916, the district name changed from Union to Manteca, and the school was often called Manteca Grammar. The 10-room building, which provided housing in the basement for Principal J.M. Luck and his wife, burned in 1948. Students studied in the American Legion Hall, Festa do Divino Espirito Santo de Manteca (FESM) Hall, and Manteca Ripon Pentecost Society (MRPS) Hall until 1950, when the new school was constructed (below). The school ceased to operate as a public grammar school in 1995, when Joshua Cowell School was built.

In 1915, a total of 25 children began attending Golden West School, constructed on North Union Road between Lathrop and French Camp Roads. The land was donated by F. Cavalero. Children transferred to Yosemite or Lindbergh in 1940–1941 when the school closed. This photograph shows the class of 1935.

Latin for "truth," Veritas School was established in 1916. One of the first trustees was the colorful A.C. Finch; he referred to students as "little hyenas" that should be fenced. Two classrooms were added in 1925 and 1931. In 1957, when the school closed, children transferred to Nile Garden.

The last of the "pioneer schools," Lindbergh Grammar School was established in 1928 in the 300 block of East North Street. The school was dedicated in honor of Charles Lindbergh, who had just completed his historic Good Will Tour. In 1971, the school was deemed unsafe to continue as a state-funded grammar school. Today, the site serves as a community center for adult education.

Bus No. 2, pictured between 1922 and 1924, was the first in the fleet for the Manteca Union High School. In 1920, nineteen local men procured the money to build temporary wooden structures for the first high school in Manteca on the present site of Manteca High School.

The first Manteca High School (Union High School), built around 1920, consisted of temporary wooden buildings. Up until then, students traveled to Stockton for higher education. Initially, two classrooms, a study hall, and a library were constructed, which were not waterproof or soundproof. Since natural light was insufficient in the buildings, electric lights were required. Additions began in 1922 in the Mission style with solid oak doors, hardwood floors, rooms heated with a furnace, telephone lines, a bell system, a 550-seat auditorium, and a gym. The gym was actually located above the pit of the auditorium. Although a net was placed to keep rogue balls from falling, balls and a student fell into the pit. During World War II, 17 teachers and 250 students attended, often scheduling half-days to enable them to work in the fields and assist with the labor shortage. The old tower failed to meet earthquake standards and was demolished in 1968.

In this photograph, taken in 1923, members of the girls' high school physical training class are suited up in their uniforms getting ready to play basketball.

New Haven School, built in 1958, subsumed Summer Home, Castle, and portions of the Atlanta Districts in 1966. The school is located on Austin Road between Northland and Lathrop Roads.

Nile Garden was established around 1957 on East Nile Avenue and bounded by Union Road and Airport Way (previously Durham Ferry). Nile Garden District subsumed portions of previous districts, including Veritas.

Lincoln School was established around 1947 and subsumed portions of previous districts, including Calla. The school is located in the 700 block of East Yosemite Avenue.

East Union High School was built in 1964 one half-mile north of the previous East Union Grammar School. The first year recorded 514 students, 26 staff, and 4 counselors.

Sequoia School was part of the school boom in the 1950s and 1960s. The school is located on Sequoia Avenue and Wawona Street.

St. Anthony's students raise the flag commemorating the first day of school on September 11, 1956. The Catholic school is located on Fremont Street adjacent to the church on North Street.

The Union Church Society, comprising Emily Cowell, Luda Reynolds, and Anna Reynolds, organized the construction of the East Union Church. The wooden structure was built in 1892 on the corner of Union Road and Louise Avenue and was used continually until it was destroyed in 1937.

First Methodist Episcopal Church was constructed in 1918. The structure seated 154 people and had additional seating for 32 in the gallery. It contained three classrooms, a parlor, and six additional classrooms in the tower. It was considered the finest building in Manteca. The building, located on the corner of Sequoia and Yosemite Avenues, houses the Manteca Historical Society and Museum.

St. Paul's Federated Methodist–Union Baptist Church began after Union Chapel burned in 1925. The Baptist and Methodist pastors joined forces to create a joint federation. The necessity for new accommodations became apparent in 1950, and an anonymous member of the congregation donated three acres where the current church stands. With funding from the sale of the previous church facilities, construction of the church pictured began in 1954.

Like many others, First Brethren worshipped at the Union Chapel until moving over to the Independent Order of Odd Fellows (IOOF) Hall, Summer Home School, and private homes. Six years after the first baptism at the Salmon Ranch in 1914, construction began on the first church on Veach and Yosemite Avenues. Pastor John Wesley Platt led the congregation for 42 years. The new church, pictured here, opened in 1971 on Northgate Avenue. Today, it is Northgate Community.

The First Christian congregation began with 12 members gathering in the blacksmith shop before moving to the IOOF Hall and, finally, constructing a church of their own on North Street and Maple Avenue in 1918, with additions in 1931 and 1947 (above). In 1953, a fire destroyed portions of the church, and in 1956, the Ladies Aid Society began fund-raising for a new church. In 1966, the congregation celebrated the opening of the new complex on Louise Avenue and Union Road. (Courtesy of Everett Patrick.)

First Baptist was constructed on North Street and North Sheridan Avenue. The picture above depicts the original church, which was built around the same time as St. Paul's and St. Anthony's, before the additional facilities were constructed.

In the Atlanta area, people opened their homes for services until 1878, when two churches were erected. This church is documented as Atlanta Church and may have been the first iteration of the First Methodist Church, prior to remodeling, on Lone Tree and French Camp Roads at Five Corners.

Catholic parishioners celebrated Mass at the original St. Patrick's Church (established in 1878) until the Cowell building was rented in 1914 for services and St. Anthony's was built. Many Catholic members of the community are buried in the cemetery behind the church, known as St. John's Cemetery.

Joshua Cowell sold three acres on East Yosemite Avenue to the Catholic congregation to begin construction of a $50,000 church and refectory, dedicated on June 22, 1916. The church was overflowing, and even residents of Stockton "motored out to be present at the ceremonies," according to the June 22, 1916, edition of the *Manteca Bulletin*. A four-room school was constructed in 1955, opening in 1956 under the tutelage of the Sisters of the Precious Blood. The church in the photograph above burned to the ground on September 12, 1960. A new church was built in the current location on North Street, and the bell from the previous church was moved here. The photograph below depicts the 1961 ground-breaking ceremonies for the new church, at which "little parishioners" Mike McCleary and Cathy Reis assist. The crowd watched as a helicopter delivered the 600-pound cross to be installed on top of the church.

Three

COMMUNITY
THE TIES THAT BIND

In 1900, Manteca was still the rugged West. The town was overrun with coyotes, rabbits, squirrels, and owls. Professional squirrel killers made the rounds offering their services. Ed Powers recalls fearing leaving his wife at home, buying her a .22 rifle for safety. Upon returning home one day, he noticed hanging from the fence 18 squirrels that his wife had shot from the kitchen window.

The board of trade, a form of government for unincorporated areas, was a mixture of a city council and chamber of commerce. Promotion of the community and development of infrastructure were its primary agendas. The first board was created in 1909, consisting of F.F. Langford, F.M. Cowell, E.N. Pierce, and J. Cowell. Board members' first mission was to improve roads, followed by a request to construct a pedestrian bridge at Mossdale. They promoted irrigation, fire safety, city lighting, a sewer system, a jail, and a high school. In 1917, Manteca had grown from 300 to 1,000 people. Manteca incorporated in 1918, and the board of trade resolved to become the chamber of commerce in 1920.

During this time, Manteca Water Works was established by A. Baccilieri and was purchased by the town in 1923. Residents paid 33¢ per 1,000 gallons of water. Electricity was brought to town in 1911, announced in the *Manteca Bulletin* as "juice . . . running over the lines." The streets were lit with four arches that spanned the street, and power was dimmed at 11:00 p.m. By 1913, individuals could connect to the lines, and by 1915, Manteca was known as a well-lit city. The sewer system was completed in 1920.

During the mid- to late 19th century, mail could take up to six months for delivery overland or by way of the Isthmus of Panama. Most settlers went to French Camp or Stockton to get mail. This photograph from 1910 shows Joseph Knight transporting the mail in Manteca with his dog in tow!

Appointed by the federal government, Anna B. Dryden was Manteca's first postmaster, serving from 1915 to 1923. The position paid $1,100 per year plus rent and expenses.

The Transcontinental Railroad (1870) offered delivery in a few days from San Francisco to South San Joaquin County, and people could obtain their mail at post offices in Lathrop or Atlanta. Initially, the Lathrop route covered residents in Manteca. William Ryhiner is pictured here in 1913 with his first car (above) and with his customers from the Summer Home route on the corner of Austin Road (far left below).

In 1908, the post office was located in the Cowell and Wiggin store. While housed at the IOOF building in 1916, the safe was blown open with nitroglycerine at 2:30 a.m. Wright Oliver, the watchman, arrived on the scene. He observed a man near the post office, ordered him to stop, and then fired two shots. However, the man fled. Investigators determined a few stamps and approximately $10 were taken. This photograph shows the current structure, built on corner of South Maple Avenue and Center Street and dedicated in 1939.

This photograph of Joshua and Emily Cowell was taken around 1904 in front of their first house. Note the fire bell on the roof in the background. Fires were fought by residents with buckets, ladders, and axes forming a bucket brigade. The first organized team of volunteers, in 1915, purchased a gasoline pump to hook up to residential wells. By 1917, they had 2 hydrants, 400 feet of hose, and 2 hose carts.

There was such discord within the organization that when the town incorporated in 1918, the board refused to support the fire department, so members initiated the firemen's ball to raise funds. The 1927 LaFrance, pictured here, had a 600-gallon-per-minute pump and cost $10,750. It was not until 1958 that the city disbanded the volunteer organization and brought the department under its direction in an official capacity.

The Manteca Fire Department is shown here in the 1940s at the baseball field on North Street. The players are Spike Hennesy, Leslie Delemeter, Elmer Blodgett, Percy Toomes, Kiel Potter, O.J. Peltier (manager), Benny Falls, Jimmy Rawleigh, Clare Mitchell, Harry Graham, ? Ramos, Pete Rose, and Joe Silva.

Located in the 100 block of Sycamore Street, the original city hall was built in 1923 with private funds. The building was home to the city offices, fire department, police department, jail, court, and library. The building was sold to Aldo Brocchini and Pete Boyce once the new city complex was erected on Center Street. Brocchini and Boyce restored the building, which stands the test of time today.

This photograph, dated 1908, depicts John Southwell (white shirt) in front of the Southwell and Sutton General Store in Lathrop. In addition to being a stockholder and board member of the Bank of Manteca, Southwell was elected to the position of justice of the peace in 1910 for Castoria Township. Manteca did not have a formal courthouse, so court proceedings occurred at various locations.

Prior to the establishment of the police department in 1918, law enforcement was covered by Castoria Township's constable and a justice of the peace. Chief Tom Brockman is pictured here (middle) flanked by night patrolmen John Toupin and Manuel Asdrubel.

Pictured here are the members of the Manteca Police Babe Ruth baseball team in 1967.

Built in 1895, the San Joaquin County Hospital was on 430 acres in what is now French Camp. A nursing school operated here in the early 20th century. A new brick building was constructed in 1932, and additions were built in 1943. This hospital served the entire South County.

A plaque was erected on May 30, 1938, to commemorate the central hub that once existed at the corner of Union Road and Louise Avenue. East Union Community Church occupied one corner from 1892 until 1937, when it was demolished, and the Union Public School served students from 1857 until 1913, when it burned down. The Union Cemetery, established in 1872, still operates on the southwest corner.

Two nurses stand guard at the entrance of the hospital constructed in 1919 in response to the flu epidemic that struck in the fall of 1918. The flu spread globally and took 500,000 lives nationwide before it ended. Everyone was required to wear a mask in public or pay a fine of $100. All community activity ceased, and businesses as well as schools were closed. Classrooms were manned by teachers around the clock to care for the sick, and the city provided supplies and paid daily visits to entire families who had succumbed to the illness. The building included 18 private rooms, 2 wards, 2 bathrooms, and an operating room.

From the late 1920s to the early 1940s, this home, owned by D.E. Rawleigh, served as Manteca's hospital; minor surgeries and deliveries of babies occurred here. The home was later utilized as a residential care home.

This home, located on the northwest corner of West Center Street and Sycamore Avenue, was built around the 1930s by C.W. Forbes. In 1941, Dr. Vincent O'Connor purchased the home and had his doctor's office here. Pharmacist and mayor Cliff Parr purchased the home in 1955. (Courtesy of Ian Patrick.)

This picture shows volunteers inspecting new ambulance equipment in 1951. The Manteca District Ambulance began that year with a $2-per-year subscription.

One of the first libraries was run by Mrs. Hooper in her store. The *Manteca Bulletin* would print the list of available books, which were exchanged with Stockton once a month. Over the years, branches were operated out of private residences, and eventually, the library landed at city hall around 1924. The building above is located at 313 West Yosemite Avenue and housed the library from 1952 to 1962.

Ground-breaking ceremonies commenced in 1961 at the location of the current library, pictured here. A new addition was built in 1978. Patricia Morris Eavenson has fond memories of the first time she stepped into the building and how much natural light shown in through the vast number of windows.

Cars lined up on the 100 block of East Yosemite Avenue in front of Joshua Cowell's house for the community fair in 1915. The tree in the front yard is where the current Bank of America is located on the southeast corner of Main Street and Yosemite Avenue looking across to what was Ace Hardware for years. The population of Manteca was 370; however, 6,000 people attended this first fair.

This photograph is from the 1915 community fair, established by Mrs. D.O. Castle to generate interest in schools and agriculture. The fair rotated to Ripon (1916) and Escalon (1917) before Stockton began the county fair. The ladies pictured above are staffing the baked goods competition booth.

This early-20th-century photograph shows young boys waving flags on the right at a downtown parade. Ladies dressed in white with parasols march along the street.

This 1946 photograph of the Sportsmen's Parade shows San Joaquin County sheriff Carlos Souza waving his hat to the crowd. The buildings are located in the 300 block of West Yosemite Avenue.

Boy Scouts from the French Camp School are pictured here in 1943–1944. From left to right are (first row) E. McAlpine, E. Thurman, B. MacLane, J. Smith, C. Mufatore, D. Ashburn, C. Thurman, A. Duncan, N. Bass, unidentified, J. Lowery, J. Strait, and G. Vezaldenos; (second row) L. Judd and B. Basti. The tall man at right in the rear is Mr. Duncan, committee man. The man with overalls and Scout hat is Scoutmaster Louis Austin.

In 1958, the Jaycees caught media attention when they sent members to the state convention in Santa Cruz via a mule-driven wagon. They stopped at other clubs along the route. Pictured here are, from left to right, Dick Ochsner, Joe Freitas, and Gary Voorheis.

The Lions Follies were a hit with the community. These lovely "ladies," including John A. Mendosa, Ralph Smith, C.C. Hitchcock, and E.C. Woodruff, perform for a January 1930 fund-raiser.

Manteca holds two annual Portuguese festas, hosted by the MRPS and the FESM Halls, to celebrate the Feast of the Holy Spirit. The festivities include the crowning of a queen and her sidemaids (attendants), a parade, and serving *sopas* (a Portuguese stew) to the public. This photograph shows the queen, Laura Mendes, her sidemaids, Maryl Coelho (left) and Dorothy Cardoza Indelicato (right), and an unidentified little cape holder. (Courtesy of Sally Mendes.)

Manteca native Milo Candini (center) was signed to the New York Yankees in 1936 before being traded to the Washington Senators. He spent 8 years in the majors and 13 years in the minors, including playing with the famous 1950 Philadelphia "Whiz Kids." He is pictured here with Phil Rizzato of the Yankees and a fan.

The Manteca baseball team sits on the stoop in front of the old Yosemite School in 1916. The players pictured here are Henry Erstad, Harold Littlejohn, Kyle Potter, P.J. Peltier, Percy Toomes, Elmer Blodgett, Nelson Potter, Porky Flinn, Jimmy Rowley, Spencer Miller, and Doc Siani.

The Manteca Belles softball team is pictured here in 1939–1940 in Library Park. Members are, from left to right, (first row) unidentified, Dorothy Stone, and two unidentified; (second row) coach Benny Hooper, Ruth Cannon, Winnie Rodrigues, unidentified, and manager William R. Perry; (third row) Mary Theiler, Winifred Souza, Kate Bronzan, Muriel Miller, and Grace Dinsdale.

Manteca boxer Tillie Delnero, photographed here in 1937, was a middleweight fighter throughout California and Nevada. He completed 30 fights in his career before joining the Manteca Police Department in 1952. He retired in 1980.

On October 1, 1920, the board of trade, established in 1909, voted to become the chamber of commerce, a government entity to promote the community. This late-1920s photograph was taken on Maple Street. From left to right are (first row) Sara Mikesell, ? Miner, Beth Oliver Walters, Kate Levinton, Sadie Littlejohn, Edna Allenbaugh, Millie Huber, Carrie Wilson, ? Bringier, Mildred Forbes, Daisy Sharenbrock, and Hattie Dietz; (second row) unidentified, John A. Mendosa Sr., unidentified, E.R. Williams, William Byrd, Ed Oliver, unidentified, Louie Dalmedge, Clarence Hughes, Jack Greenberg, Achille Bacilieri, Marrow Litchfield, Frank Crabtree (police), unidentified, C.W. Forbes, unidentified, Joe Wilson, Dr. A.H. Meredith, Clyde Woods, Judge E. Douglas, unidentified, Ed Powers, two unidentified, Herman Dike, Art Paul, Dr. A.J. Whitaker, and J. Walter Graves; (third row) K.D. McBrian, four unidentified, Rev. Arthur P. Brown, R.E. Leventon, and unidentified.

Four

Commerce and Industry
Getting Down to Business

Mormons led by William Stout established a small settlement near the bend in the San Joaquin River and were the first to try their hand at irrigation, digging a ditch three quarters of a mile long. Regretfully, their short-lived colony was not to last. Joshua and Wright Cowell began a ditch system, contracting to build nine miles of waterways. However, the men abandoned the endeavor, nearly going broke in the process due to farmers refusing to buy the water. Eventually, the promise of water around 1910, when the first bonds were issued to build the South San Joaquin Irrigation District, created quite a stir, and speculators wanted to cash in on the potential success of the new town.

In an attempt to entice people, the *Manteca Enterprise* advertised that the town had two miles of cement sidewalks, good streets, a telegraph system, water, a train, and automobiles. According to Evelyn Prouty's *Manteca: Selected Chapters from Its History*, it advertised the need for "a clothing store, tailor, watchmaker, plumber, optician, druggist, lawyer, a steam laundry and moving picture show." During this period, downtown began to take shape. Most of the brick buildings along Yosemite Avenue were built at this time, and people flocked to the town to fill them. The town Joshua Cowell had always dreamed of was about to boom.

Pictured here in 1912 is downtown Manteca with M.B. Hooper's store on the northwest corner of Yosemite Avenue and Main Street. Mrs. Hooper ran the library in the store, and the "free library" sign is visible by the front entrance. The "Manteca" sign is faintly visible in the background, hanging over the street near the railroad tracks.

This c. 1918 photograph, taken from the intersection of Main Street and Yosemite Avenue, depicts downtown Manteca. The importance of the creamery industry can be seen in at least three storefronts offering ice cream within a few feet of each other.

Originally, the Manteca Creamery was a skimming station established in 1896 by Joshua Cowell and operated by a cooperative of dairymen. There, whole milk was separated from the cream shipped to the Bay Area—in excess of 100 gallons of cream daily (8,500 pounds of butter). The cooperative was sold to Ed Powers in 1906 and was opened to the public for the first time by Morgansen and Nielson in 1914. By the 1920s, dairy was the largest industry in the area, and with mechanization and additions, the creamery was producing 395,000 pounds of butter per year and supplying Army bases during World War II. Shortly after the war, the Manteca Creamery ceased butter production and focused on ice cream, creating a hub for families and teenagers who hold the Manteca Creamery near and dear in memory. This photograph is from 1933.

This c. 1920 photograph shows delivery trucks lined up in front of the Manteca Cream and Butter Company (also known as the Manteca Creamery Co.).

This picture was taken on opening day of the Manteca Creamery, a combination ice cream parlor and sandwich shop. It was added onto the front of the previous Manteca Cream and Butter Company. The early creamery was the first industry in Manteca, which gave rise to the name of the town.

This c. 1920 photograph shows the delivery cars of the Manteca Cream and Butter Company. Note the milk cans loaded up.

This photograph, taken around 1920, shows milk cans at the loading and weigh station. One of the owners, Floyd Richards, is second from the left.

The first cheese factory in Manteca was established in 1921. Kraft Foods Company began in 1935 on Poplar Street prior to moving to this location, which was built in 1927 on Oak Street. The company closed its doors in 1977, ironically citing the lack of a milk supply. Kraft Foods employees are pictured here during a shift change in 1961.

Claus Spreckels began his career in the San Joaquin Valley, building the San Francisco & San Joaquin Railroad. In 1896, he filed the articles of incorporation for Spreckels Sugar Company, and by 1901, he had expanded to eight plants. In 1916, about 7,000 acres of sugar beets were planted by more than 50 farmers. The population that year was 371, and the number grew to 567 after Spreckels decided to build his plant here.

After the sugar shortage of World War I, domestic sugar demands created a new industry. Beginning locally in 1915, the sugar beet industry was a successful endeavor, providing yearly employment and seasonal work. In 1916, the Spreckels Sugar Company constructed a facility, followed by a new factory—outfitted with the latest equipment, office buildings, clubhouse, landscaped grounds, and a row of company houses on Yosemite Avenue—in 1918.

The local newspaper originated as the *Irrigation Bulletin* and transitioned to the *Manteca Bulletin* in 1914; however, the official name change did not appear on the front page until 1917. George Murphy Sr., pictured around 1915, took over the newspaper in 1923.

The *Manteca Bulletin*'s original building was located on the north side of the 300 block of West Yosemite Avenue. The newspaper operated out of this building from 1912 to about 1956.

Pictured are Harry Callander, George Murphy Sr., and shop foreman Clark Whelan in the back print shop of the *Manteca Bulletin*. This photograph dates to 1927, when the *Bulletin* was located at 309 West Yosemite Avenue. The Murphy name became synonymous with the paper. George Murphy Jr. became the sole proprietor in 1949.

The Manteca Bulletin Building, located at the corner of East Yosemite Avenue and Fremont Street, previously housed the Keppel Brothers Hardware store. The *Bulletin* moved to this location around 1956, remaining until 1965. The *Bulletin* moved back in 1970.

The *Manteca Bulletin* used to be delivered by kids who wanted to earn a few bucks. These young boys are out on their route in the 1960s. Marty Harris is pictured in the center with the baseball cap.

George Murphy Jr. is pictured here with the first lady of the United States, Eleanor Roosevelt, as he is presented with an award for his military service.

George Murphy Jr. was a survivor of the USS *Oklahoma* (below), which sank on December 7, 1941, in Pearl Harbor. On that day, 2,402 people died from the attack, including 429 from the *Oklahoma*.

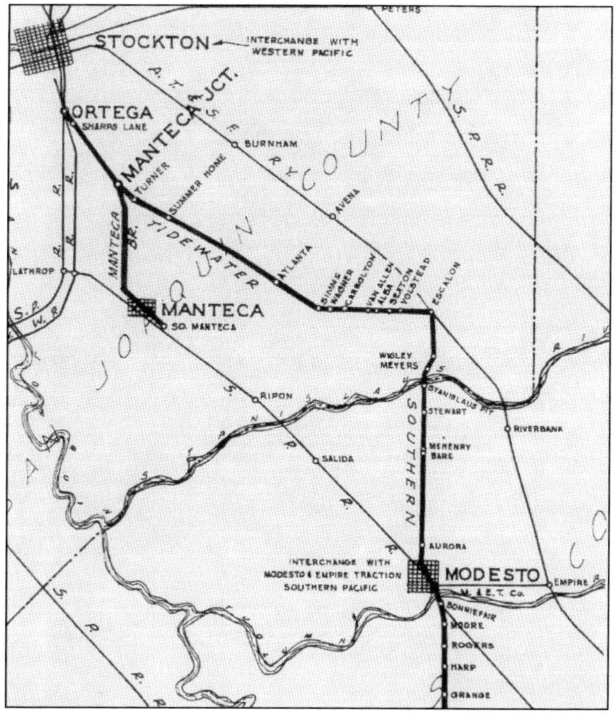

The Tidewater Southern rail route map, trending from Stockton to Modesto (around 1912), depicts the spur entering Manteca, which was completed in 1918. The line offered transportation to local residents as well as for shipping products and supplies to and from the canneries and Spreckels. The route from Stockton to Modesto took 65 minutes on the "Toonerville Trolley," the nickname given to the Tidewater Southern.

Manteca Station, pictured here in 1962, was located on Yosemite Avenue near Library Park. The Tidewater Southern Railroad traveled 33.1 miles between Stockton and Modesto, with 36 stations. In 1931, a round trip cost $1. A special destination, reserved by people throughout the county, was Salmon's Grove on French Camp Road, where the platform was decorated with Japanese lanterns and dancing lasted all night long.

The Tidewater Southern Locomotive No. 32 is depicted here in the 1930s. In 1916, a total of 24 trains ran daily from Stockton to Modesto. With the advent of the automobile, the number of trains declined to 8 in 1932. While passenger trains became part of the distant past, steam engines from Western Pacific were often called in to assist with the demanding freight loads. Goods were still being hauled twice a day into the 1980s.

This photograph shows men laying track for the Tidewater Southern. The railroad track was dismantled in the 1990s and replaced with the Tidewater Bikeway, a recreational trail that extends from Lathrop Road to Spreckels Avenue.

Two points of interest are celebrated here. California Historic Landmark (CHL) No. 437 recognizes the first boat to navigate up the San Joaquin River from San Francisco in 1846. The first ferry on the San Joaquin River was established here by John Doak and Jacob Bonsell and later purchased by Capt. William S. Moss. CHL No. 787 commemorates the last spike that joined the Transcontinental Railroad with the San Joaquin River railroad bridge at Mossdale Landing. (Courtesy of Bank of Stockton.)

The First State Bank of Manteca was established in 1911. A new building was erected to house the First National Bank (1917), later the Liberty Bank of America (1927), on the southeast corner of Yosemite Avenue and Main Street. The name changed to Bank of Italy, and finally Bank of America, in 1930. The building pictured here was demolished, and the current building was constructed in 1968.

The San Joaquin Telephone Company, later the Continental Telephone, was housed next to the old city hall on Manteca Avenue. Dial telephones were introduced in 1957 with a "how to" article printed in the *Bulletin*, and a new emergency number, TAlbot 3-2101, took effect on December 14 of that same year. TAlbot 3 was a prefix assigned to all Manteca subscribers. This photograph dates to the 1960s.

This photograph shows ladies operating the switchboard at the San Joaquin Telephone Company in the 1920s.

M.B. Hooper Hardware, Groceries, and Drygoods is pictured here around 1912. Hooper's store was on the northwest corner of the intersection of Main Street and Yosemite Avenue.

The clubhouse of Hooper and Callander Contractors is pictured here around 1912. The boys are Benny Hooper and George Callander, the son of M.B. Hooper and brother of Harry Callander from the *Manteca Bulletin*.

J.J. and Vina Overshiner opened Manteca Cash Store, the first retail store and butcher shop, followed by a blacksmith shop, in 1898 on West Yosemite Avenue near the railroad tracks. There is some information that states this was a general store and barbershop. The Overshiners petitioned for the railroad depot after the skimming station started. J.J. served as a councilman in 1925 and as mayor in 1930.

The Rochdale General Store operated as a co-op and was founded in 1905. When the venture began to fail, Joshua Cowell took over management, operating it until the investors were paid. The location also served as a post office for a period. The meat department continued to conduct business after the store closed.

Lauritson's General Merchandise, pictured here around 1920, was located on East Yosemite and Lincoln Avenues. The building was erected by Thomas C. Lauritson in 1916. The store sold every commodity from groceries to home goods. Gas pumps were installed, a meat market was added, and an icehouse was established in 1925. Customers paid their bills annually after the harvest. George Lauritson, the son, went on to own Manteca Variety with his wife, Kathryn, from 1939 to 1976.

The Manteca Meat Market was located in the 200 block of West Yosemite Avenue. Pictured here in the 1920s, the building had multiple functions. The trade union occupied the upstairs, the Manteca Social Club utilized the building, and it was used as a school when East Union burned in 1914.

Dante's Market (possibly Manteca Meat Market) was located in the 200 block of West Yosemite Avenue. It was owned by Dante Bernacchi and family from the late 1920s to the 1930s.

Raymond Honodel was a pharmacist who served Manteca from 1929 to 1975. Honodel's Drugs was located in the 100 block of West Yosemite Avenue. He used to hang pictures of all the local men and women serving from World War II through Vietnam. He was one of the initial investors in Doctors Hospital and a supporter of the Manteca Historical Society. Raymond Honodel lived to be 101 years old!

Equally important in Manteca's history of pop culture was the Scoop Newsstand and Fountain, located on the northeast corner of Yosemite and Sycamore Avenues. This photograph is from the 1940s and depicts owner Lillian Merjano on the left.

This photograph shows daily life as it would have appeared in downtown Manteca in the 1950s. The other drugstore, Manteca Drugs, is shown here. The Turner Hardware Company is located in the IOOF building.

Home Lumber Company, photographed here in 1919, was located at the intersection of South Main Street and Moffat Boulevard. Initially owned by J. Boberg, then R.P. Fuller, it became Diamond Match Co. This delivery truck was known as an "auto-car." The barrels on the roof may have been for fire.

Edward O. Perry and a passenger are seen here in 1910 with his early-day racer at the Oakland Speedway. Perry operated a garage in town on Moffat Boulevard.

The Eastside Garage, next door to the Village Smithy, supplied Shell gasoline. This photograph was taken around 1928.

Located in the 500 block of East Yosemite Avenue, the Village Smithy, photographed in 1929, sold farm equipment by the proprietors, Branco and Rocha. Note the phone number as 187-M. Perched in the front of the building, the eagle statue, known as "Old Abe," was not only the symbol of the Wisconsin 8th Infantry during the Civil War but also the trade symbol of the J.I. Case Co., manufacturers of construction and agricultural equipment.

The new Branco's Tractor & Equipment Co. store is pictured here with the "Old Abe" eagle statue of the J.I. Case Co. mounted over the entrance. The date on the building is 1945.

John A. and Mary A. Mendosa, photographed here in 1922, owned Mendosa's Menswear and Shoe Store, located at 143 Yosemite Avenue. When the new post office was built in 1939, the Mendosas contributed a collection of 45 uncanceled US commemorative stamps to be reclaimed by their neediest descendant. The stamps are contained in the cornerstone of the building.

John August Mendosa immigrated from the island of Madeira and married Mary E. Gomes from the same island. In 1916, the Mendosas opened Mendosa's Menswear, which served Manteca for 74 years! The store had a shoe department and a cobbler, John Pinto. This ad was featured in the *Manteca Bulletin* in 1922.

This photograph of the Model Laundry (later the Domestic Laundry) was taken in 1923 in the 100 block of North Maple Avenue. From left to right are Mary Solami, Michelina Cala, Mayme Cronin, Irma Larson, and Sarah Cosgriff. Cala was the mother of Sadie Cabral (who became the owner of Sadie's Salon, which is still operating today), and Cosgriff was the mother of Babe Gatto.

An early tow truck is pictured in front of the Main Highway Garage on South Highway 99.

One of the mainstays of Manteca industry is the Delicato Family Vineyards, located on the frontage road of Highway 99. Founder Gaspare Indelicato, who emigrated from Italy, chose Manteca because it reminded him of Sicily, where his family grew wine grapes for centuries. This photograph depicts the beginning of the winery with the Sam Jasper Winery Wholesale and Retail Liquor Dealer.

Gaspare Indelicato founded the Delicato Family Vineyards in 1924 with his three sons. Three generations later, the family still owns and operates the winery. Today, the company has an international presence.

This photograph is of the Indelicato children in 1937.

This c. 1918 photograph, taken on Oak Street, depicts Achille Baccilieri (far left) with Cesare and Lucia Candini and their children, from left to right, Ramo, Robert, Frank, Stella, and Louie (note that Milo Candini was not born yet). Baccilieri, founder of the area's first winery and owner of a waterworks, was an uncle to the Candinis.

Manteca Winery, on Oak Street, was founded by A. Baccilieri. The building was constructed in 1909 with Carnegie bricks from the old factory near Tracy. Today, the structure is the oldest brick building in Manteca. The Baccilieri name is mispelled on the original building seen here.

The Manteca Canning Company was founded by A. Baccilieri, T.A. Nelson, F.M. Cowell, and Louis Vistica in 1914. The entrepreneurs realized the need for a plant to process the local produce, and the old winery was expanded on Oak Street. The first batch of Manteca Lady tomatoes was processed that year, and it was not long until soldiers in France during World War I were eating a taste of home.

This photograph shows the crew of the Manteca Canning Company. The Manteca Canning Company incorporated in 1914, and people came from throughout the valley to celebrate. Peaches from W.W. Cowell's orchard were the first items to be processed and canned. Over 19,000 cases of fruits and vegetables were produced the first year, growing to 200,000 cases by 1918! As the

company expanded, the demand for labor increased. Small cottages were built southeast of the cannery for seasonal workers. As the area declined into a shanty town in the 1930s, the area became known as Hoovertown.

The El Rey Theater was built in 1937 in the 100 block of East Yosemite Avenue. Fire destroyed the El Rey Theater in 1975. Ironically, the featured film that night was *The Towering Inferno.* The original poster is on display in the Manteca Historical Society and Museum.

Five

Agriculture
The Sandy Loam of South County

Many came for the gold, but they stayed for the agriculture. Prior to coming west, most settlers had been engaged in some agricultural pursuit. The South County offered two soil types divided geographically by French Camp Road—moisture-retaining adobe to the north and sandy loam to the south. Prior to irrigation, settlers realized the potential of the sandy loam and embarked on planting dry farming crops, such as wheat, barley, and oats.

Cattle provided the main agricultural economy until the 1860s. Drought devastated the industry, and ranchers began to plant grain in abundance. Farmers achieved great success, catapulted by the Stockton gangplow. The Stockton gangplow improved on original designs and was a major development over the "foot burner," or single, plows of the past. In 1890, it took eight to ten man-hours to produce 20 bushels (one acre) of wheat. This cut the time of previous efforts, which required 50 to 60 hours man-hours to obtain the same results.

Initially, crops were shipped via wagon or waterway. With the arrival of the Central Pacific Railroad around 1870, a shipment for an entire crop went from weeks to one or two days. During the turn of the century, alfalfa, melons, grapes, and almonds dominated the agricultural scene. With the formation of the irrigation district, Manteca became known as the District of Diversified Crops.

The alfalfa boom, brought on by irrigation, began the dairy industry and the Manteca known today. Spreckels sugar beets and tomatoes for the cannery provided a means for both agricultural pursuits and employment. Finally, in the 1920s, the almond orchards, which surround the town, became the principal crop.

Beginning with the Tulloch Ditch System, 47 miles of ditches from Knights Ferry to the South County delivered water to 3,000 acres under the San Joaquin Water Company of H.W. Cowell and N.S. Harrold. The Wright Irrigation Law was the impetus for the development of the SSJID, established in 1909. Located in the 200 block of North Main Street, the SSJID Building was constructed in 1922, housing the district until 1968, when it moved to Highway 120.

The South San Joaquin Irrigation District began construction of a 400-foot dam on the Stanislaus River, two and a half miles above Knights Ferry, in 1912. Named after the "Father of the South San Joaquin Irrigation District," Benjamin A. Goodwin, the president of the board of directors for the district, the dam was completed in 1913. The *Stockton Record* noted that the dedication ceremony, overseen by Gov. Hiram Johnson, brought out every auto in the county on the road to Knights Ferry. According to Evelyn Prouty's *Manteca: Selected Chapters from Its History*, the picnic grounds were crowded with "927 autos, 107 motorcycles, and over 100 buggies" and 4,000 people. Three hundred miles of ditches, tunnels, and flumes were constructed to bring water to Manteca. On August 13, 1913, the first farmer to receive water was E.N. Pierce, SSJID secretary, on his ranch located at the southeast corner of Austin Road and Highway 120. Irrigation began in earnest the following year.

The Stanislaus and San Joaquin Rivers pose a threat to valley residents, particularly farmers, and a series of levees surrounds the town. Several floods were documented in the 19th century, claiming lives and sweeping away settlements. In the 20th century, the worst flooding occurred in 1950, submerging farmland and causing erosion and deposition. The remains of livestock were found throughout the area. This photograph shows farmland inundated with waters in the 1950s.

One of the oldest structures in Manteca is the sole surviving barn out at the Zinc House on Highway 120 and Wagner Road. This was originally a hotel and stage stop for travelers heading to the mines, including the Fisher Stage Line. Most notably, Pres. Ulysses S. Grant stayed here on his way to Knights Ferry. The barn and granary, constructed in about 1863, housed grain for shipment. (Courtesy of Ian and Everett Patrick.)

Elizabeth Willis was the first San Joaquin County home advisor. Here, she is in front of the company car. The program was a cooperative effort between the US government, the University of California, and San Joaquin County farmers. Advisors shared farming techniques, scientific methods, advice regarding plants and animals, housekeeping tips, youth education, and summer programs and addressed labor shortages. The program was essential during World War I and World War II.

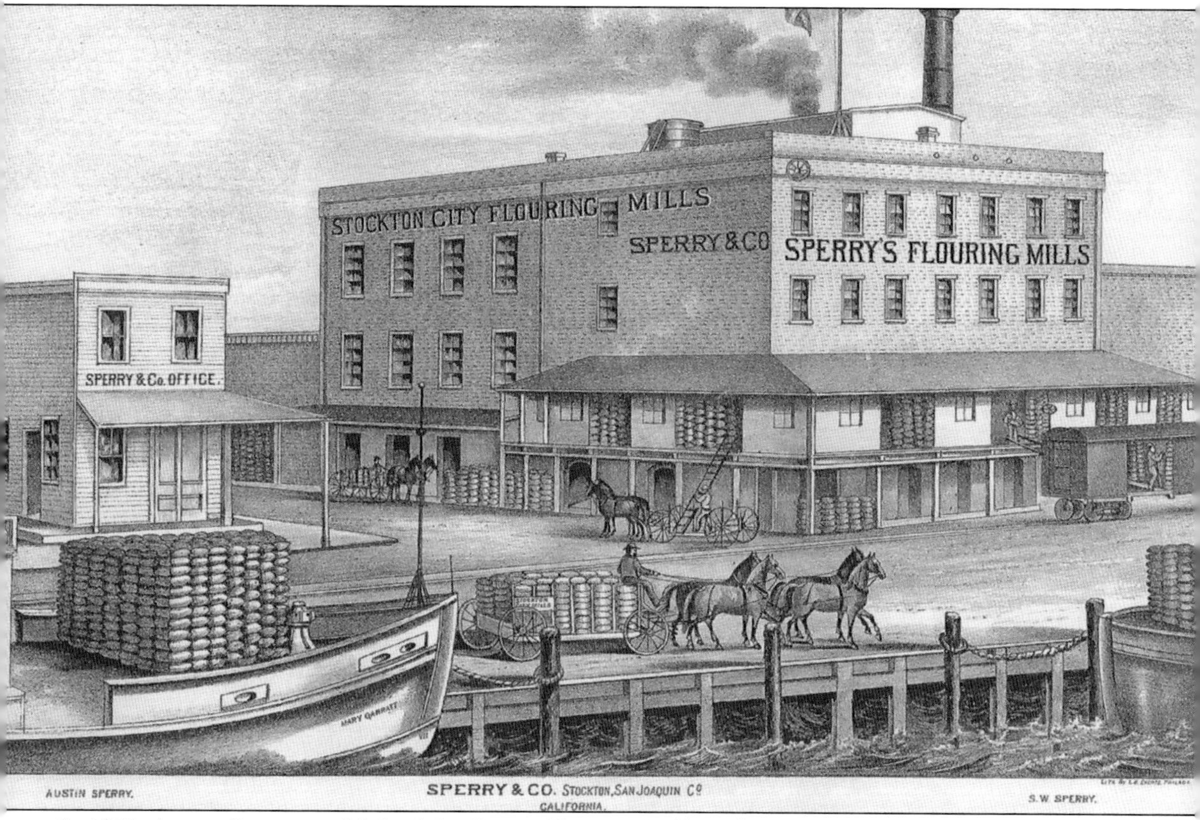

In 1852, Austin Sperry established the Sperry Flouring Mill on the corner of West Weber Avenue and Madison Street in Stockton. Until the railroad was built, it took weeks for a grain crop to be transported by a team of horses or via waterway from Manteca to Stockton. Grain was shipped to the mill and distributed internationally in the 1860s; up to 19 ships were ready to be deployed in the Stockton channel for every shipment.

The Sperry brothers were one of the first families to till the soil in Manteca. Arriving in 1852, the brothers worked their own lands as well as an additional 8,000 acres, reaping $30,000 per year in grain profits. J.C. and H.D. Sperry owned property adjacent to the Southern Pacific Railroad on West Yosemite Avenue, next to Joshua Cowell.

The 160-acre Tinnin Ranch, depicted here in 1906, was located at the north end of Tinnin Road and Woodward Road.

An L.L. Miller harvester, ground-powered and pulled by a 20-mule team, was commonly used prior to irrigation in the South County. Harvesters were priced between $1,200 to $2,000 and could be pulled by up to a 30-mule team, each animal valued up to $200.

This photograph of an eight-mule team and gangplow was taken at the Middle Ranch of brothers Noah and Peter Clapp. The ranch was affectionately known as Summer Home and consisted of 1,000 acres near the current New Haven School. The man operating the jerk line is J.J. Overshiner. J.J.'s wife, Vina, and son Edgar are seated in the buggy.

A threshing crew is depicted here in 1898. In 1880, the largest wheat crop in the world was produced in San Joaquin County, resulting in over 3 million bushels! It would take 1,024 freight-train cars to move that much grain.

Joseph Fassler, a Swiss emigrant, operated an impressive dairy complex at the west end of Louise Avenue. Two hundred and fifty dairy cows produced 600 gallons of milk shipped to San Francisco daily. The dairy farm, photographed here in 1913, was situated on 750 acres.

Moffat's Feed Lot, pictured here in the 1950s, was located adjacent to the Spreckels Sugar Factory. Manteca was known for its aroma associated with the feed lots.

Delphino Perry emigrated from the Azores at 16 years old. In 1925, he started a dairy and farm, the beginnings of George Perry and Sons, Inc. George Perry Sr. is pictured here with his daughter Carolyn at their fruit stand in the 1940s. Perry was dubbed the "Pumpkin King" in *People* magazine (1982). Today, this family operation is one of the largest shippers and handlers of watermelons and pumpkins in California.

The Manteca Bean Company was located at Grant Avenue and Moffat Boulevard across from the Tidewater Southern Railway depot. The facility later housed the Golden Grain Macaroni Co., a subsidiary of Quaker Oats.

This advertisement from Glenn Kahl celebrates the Annual Pumpkin Festival of Manteca. Originally located at Library Park and organized by local growers, the festivities moved to Main Street, returning to their original location in recent years. Kahl, the preeminent photographer of Manteca, created many such images using Manteca as the backdrop.

L.L. Miller, farmer and inventor, made many contributions to the almond industry. He assisted with the development of the Caterpillar tractor while working at Holt Brothers in Stockton and developed an almond huller. This photograph is dated 1926.

Almonds were introduced in the area in the 1890s; however, the crop really took off in the 1920s. The trees thrived in the sandy loam, producing 1,000 pounds of almonds per acre. This photograph shows one of L.L. Miller's Caterpillars tilling the soil in one of the early orchards located on his property.

L.L. Miller sold the patent to this almond huller to the Capp brothers of Stockton. These machines, photographed around 1926, are essentially the same hullers sold today.

This photograph from L.L. Miller's ranch (East Highway 120) was taken during the almond harvest in 1919. Harvest time was a family affair. In 1908, Laurence Lee Miller (born around 1879), son of Milton and Sarah Margaret Maxwell, married Nellie May Goodwin (born in 1883), daughter of Benjamin Goodwin and Mary Eleanor Clapp. All were early pioneer families. The Millers had four children, L. Duane, Kent G., Marvin L., and Muriel.

One of the first buildings in Manteca was A. Baccilieri's Manteca Winery. Grapes were delivered in wooden gondolas via the railroad. This 1912 photograph, taken facing southeast towards Main Street, shows a barn in the background belonging to Ed Powers.

A family is photographed here in the 1920s during the tomato harvest on South Manteca Road. Manteca was dubbed "Tomatoville" at one time. The first operation to cash in on the surplus of produce grown with the assistance of the new irrigation was the Manteca Canning Company, opened in 1914; it was running around the clock by the second year. Manteca Packing Company opened in 1917, and two additional operations opened by 1918.

Fourteen Russian families from British Columbia and Saskatchewan settled in 1924 on 140 acres at the south end of Castle Road. They formed a cooperative, raising grapes marketed under the name Ruscol, short for the "Russian Colony." The children attended Castle School with Italians, Greeks, Mexicans, and Portuguese. The houses had basements for food storage, some had steam rooms known as *banyas*, and the community had a prayer home. These immigrants were part of a religious sect of Russian dissenters who were known as Doukhobors, extreme Christian pacifists. The photograph above was taken in the 1930s during the apricot harvest. Below is a more recent photograph of the still-standing religious prayer building. (Below, courtesy of Everett Patrick.)

William and Mary Dimotakis emigrated from Crete. The Dimotakis family farm was a self-sufficient homestead near Manteca, operating here between 1935 and 1942. The Greek family grew an amazing variety of crops, including figs, apricots, peaches, loquats, dates, oranges, lemons, limes, mulberries, melons, grapes, peas, beans, zucchini, avocados, olives, pecans, walnuts, and almonds. The farm included an olive oil plant, a dairy, an aviary, livestock, and a wood-burning oven for baking bread. They were also beekeepers and harvested honey. The weekends were a time for social gatherings, which often included roasting a lamb or goat on a spit. (Both, courtesy of the Library of Congress.)

Six

Manteca Today
And the Beat Goes On

Manteca has been dubbed "the Family City." In 2015, Manteca was in the top 10 cities in the nation for growth, attracting people from metropolitan areas with what many consider to be small-town values and sense of community. City leaders have strived to balance the exponential growth Manteca faces with the expansion of the residential, commercial, and industry base. The population of Manteca in 2019 is around 80,000.

Manteca has a variety of recreational activities, including Big League Dreams Sports Park, a top-rated BMX track, a skate park, an 18-hole municipal championship golf course, a four-mile-long recreation path, and 400 acres of neighborhood and community parks. The Flags over Manteca began in honor of 9/11 and is an impressive volunteer effort that displays 2,400 flags to celebrate patriotic holidays throughout the year, and there is a weekly farmers' market celebrating agricultural heritage. The chamber of commerce calendar is packed every month with events. There are countless parades and fairs throughout the year, including the Manteca Pumpkin Fair, Portuguese festas, Manteca Crossroads Street Faire, Veteran's and Memorial Day remembrances, and parades at the Fourth of July and Christmas, just to name a few. The best parts of Manteca are the traditions that are carried on and the cultural and local legacies that are celebrated. Those are the cornerstones of the community.

Crossroads, the first of the mural collection designed by David Gordon in 2003, is located at the intersection of Yosemite Avenue and Main Street. The mural replicates the same view of the intersection from 1918. The Manteca Mural Society was established in 2002 and currently has 32 individual themed murals throughout the city. Most feature local historic landmarks, buildings, events, and citizens. (Courtesy of Ian Patrick.)

The Manteca Ripon Pentecost Society and the Festa do Divino Espirito Santo de Manteca Portuguese organizations were established in 1919 and 1931, respectively. In 2019, the MRPS celebrates its centennial with Chris Teicheira serving as the president, carrying on the family tradition. His grandfather Manuel Teicheira and father, Richard Teicheira, served as previous presidents. In this photograph, Chris Teicheira is flanked by sidemaids Elsie (left) and Lela Patrick. (Courtesy of Melinda Pacheco Patrick.)

This photograph from 1979 shows Richard Teicheira (front) on the family dairy. Dairy farming is still big business in Manteca with generations of families carrying on the tradition. The Teicheiras own two dairies, Manuel Teicheira Dairy on Perrin Road and Frank T. Teicheira Dairy on Airport Road, currently operated by Richard and Frank Jr., respectively. (Courtesy of Chris Teicheira.)

Approximately 2,000 acres around Manteca produce 47,400 tons of pumpkins, representing 88 percent of the commercially grown pumpkins in the state. George Perry and Sons and Del Osso Farms are producers today, and Manteca carries on the tradition of celebrating the crop with the Pumpkin Fair at Library Park, a tradition that began in 1966 with the Manteca Pumpkin Growers. Pictured here in 2016 are, from left to right, Miss Young Pumpkin Fair Emma Yeszin, Miss Pumpkin Fair Christina Arcos, Pumpkin Fair Ambassador Gabe Ortega, and Miss Teen Pumpkin Fair Ashlynn Nussbaumer. (Courtesy of Jennifer Yeszin.)

The 23rd annual Crossroads Street Faire was held in 2019. The event, held downtown on Yosemite Avenue and Main Street, attracts between 30,000 and 40,000 people over the weekend. The fair is held in the same location as the community fair, which took place in 1915 in the heart of downtown. (Courtesy of *Manteca Bulletin*.)

The South San Joaquin Irrigation District has been serving the areas surrounding Escalon, Manteca, and Ripon since 1909. Manteca is still prime farmland consisting of fruit and nut orchards, field crops, vineyards, dairies, and pastures all irrigated by SSJID. (Courtesy of Ian Patrick.)

San Joaquin County was rated the top wine grape–growing region in the state in 2017; growers produced over $2.5 billion of the crop. Delicato Family Vineyards, located on Highway 99 and French Camp Road, has been family owned and operated since 1924. It is the largest year-round agricultural employer in the Manteca area and is rated as one of the top 10 wineries in the country. (Courtesy of Ian Patrick.)

Continuing the tradition of an old-fashioned butcher shop and deli, Fagundes has been serving Manteca since 1976. Fagundes has strong roots in the Portuguese community and has been locally owned since its inception. Today, Fagundes Meats and Catering is owned by Frank Teixeira. The meat market is located on Jason Street. (Courtesy of Ian Patrick.)

Tipton's Stationery and Gifts, Inc., on West Yosemite and Maple Avenues, has been a staple in the community since 1961. The store has the old-fashioned feel of a specialty department store, providing everything from wedding and event items to dinnerware and office supplies. This unique gift shop is family owned and operated by Bea Bowlsby and her daughter Brenda Franklin in the c. 1917 Pezzoni and Wells Building. (Courtesy of Ian Patrick.)

Big League Dreams is the culmination of a vision that two former baseball players and entrepreneurs had in bringing a big-league playing experience to the average player. The stadium facilitates the tradition of the great American pastime. In 2006, the complex was built on 31 acres on Milo Candini Drive in honor of local legend and major-league baseball player Milo Candini. (Courtesy of Ian Patrick.)

Bass Pro Shop, located in the Orchard Valley Promenade, opened its doors in 2008. It is the biggest tourist attraction around for sports enthusiasts of all types. Shortly after opening, 2.7 million people passed through the doors in 2009. (Courtesy of Ian Patrick.)

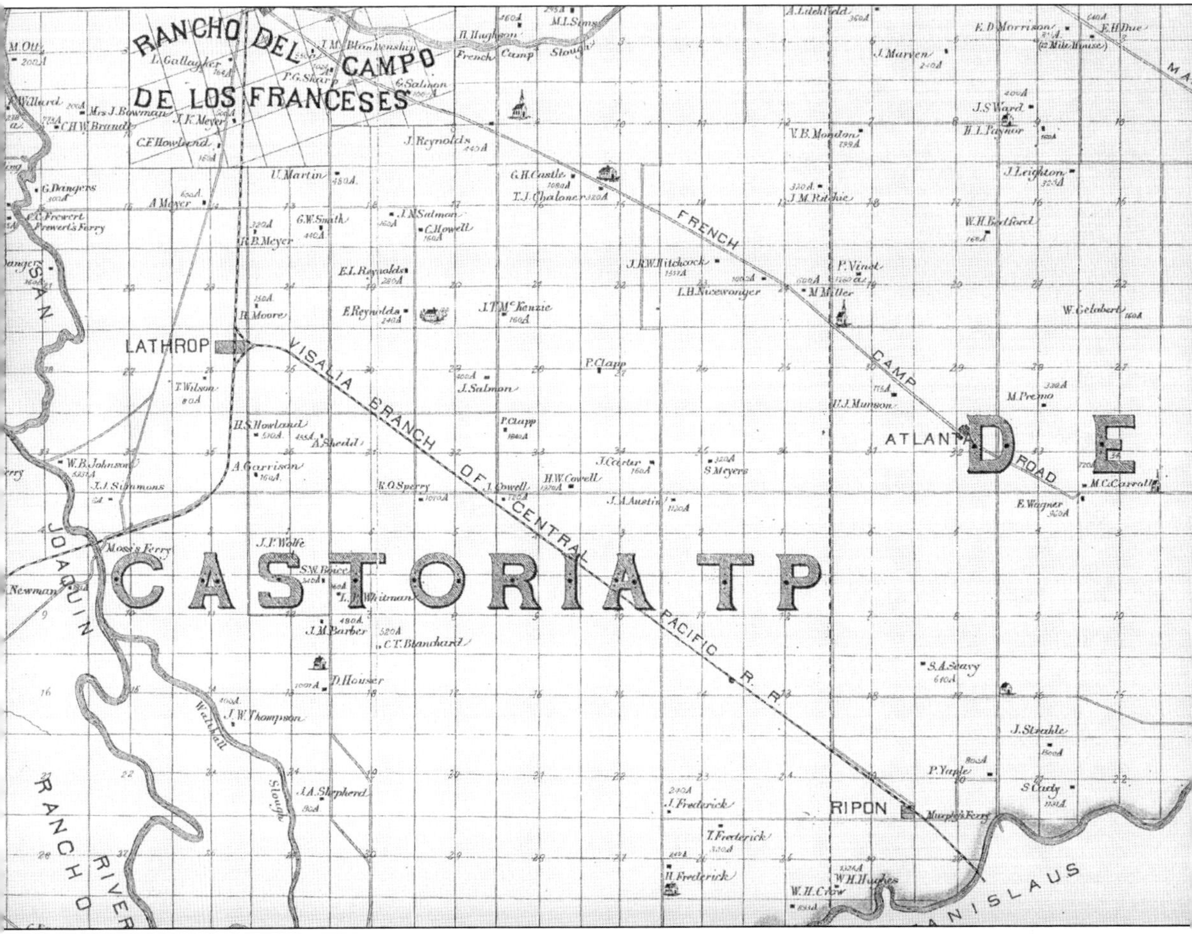

The Castoria Township map depicted here, from the late 19th to early 20th century, shows many of the original land owners and pioneer families. When California became a state in 1850, San Joaquin County was one of the original 27 counties. Castoria is one of 11 townships that make up San Joaquin County.

Bibliography

Albano, Rose. "The Manteca Russian Colony." Doukhobor Genealogy Website. www.doukhobor.org/Manteca.html.

Alfieri, Elsie. *Unforgettable Atlanta.* Atlanta, CA: Arthur Clark Company, 2002.

Ancestry.com.

Coon, Alice B. *Manteca: The Story of a Town.* Manteca, CA: Manteca Historical Society, 1943.

"El Rey Was Manteca's Grand Dame Back in 1937." *Manteca Bulletin*, December 26, 2014.

Findagrave.com.

Hillman, Raymond W., and Leonard A. Covello. *Cities and Towns of San Joaquin County since 1847.* Fresno: Panorama West Books, 1985.

Jones, Terry L., and Kathryn A. Klar, eds. *California Prehistory: Colonization, Culture, and Complexity.* Lanham, MD: Rowman and Littlefield, 2007.

Kahl, Glenn. "MDA: Serving Since 1951." *Manteca Bulletin*, January 10, 2019.

Latta, Frank F., ed. *Handbook of Yokuts Indians.* Bakersfield, CA: Kern County Museum, 1949.

Manteca Centennial, 1918–2018. Manteca, CA: Manteca Bulletin, 2018.

Moratto, Michael J. *California Archaeology.* Orlando: Academic Press, 2004

Patrick, Melinda Pacheco, et al. *Archaeological Survey Report for the Pacific Gas and Electric Company, Wheeler Ridge Substation, Kern County, California.* Patrick GIS Group, Inc., Manteca, California. Mountain View, CA: TRC Solutions, 2014.

Prouty, Evelyn. *Manteca: Selected Chapters from Its History.* Manteca, CA: Manteca Bulletin, 1980.

"Pumpkin Fun Rolls into Manteca." *Oakdale Leader*, September 25, 2018.

"San Joaquin County, CA—Index to Federal Land Patents." California Land Patents Database, June 14, 2008. files.usgwarchives.net/ca/sanjoaquin/land/.

"Smoky Times for Old Winery." *Manteca Bulletin*, April 10, 2011.

Spencer, Horace A. *The Railroads of San Joaquin County.* Manteca, CA: San Joaquin County School District, 1976.

Stuart, David R. "The Native Peoples of San Joaquin County: Indian Pioneers, Immigrants, Innovators, Freedom Fighters, and Survivors." *San Joaquin Historian*, Summer 2016.

Thompson, Thomas H., and Albert A. West. *History of San Joaquin County, California, with Illustrations.* Berkeley, CA: Thompson and West, 1879.

Wallace, William J. "Northern Valley Yokuts," in *Handbook of North American Indians*, edited by William C. Sturtevant, 8:462–470. Washington, DC: Smithsonian Institution, 1978.